"Let's see if we can work out

exactly what he was painting."

Original Korean text by Seon-hye Jang
Illustrations by Jae-seon Ahn
Korean edition © Aram Publishing

This English edition published by big & SMALL in 2016
by arrangement with Aram Publishing
English text edited by Scott Forbes
English edition © big & SMALL 2016

Distributed in the United States and Canada by
Lerner Publishing Group, Inc.
241 First Avenue North
Minneapolis, MN 55401 U.S.A.
www.lernerbooks.com

ISBN: 978-1-925249-09-5

Printed in Korea

Seen from a Distance

THE ART OF MONET

Written by Seon-hye Jang

Illustrated by Jae-seon Ahn

Edited by Scott Forbes

It would be hard to draw a magnificent garden like this in a small sketchbook, wouldn't it?

Detail from *Women in the Garden* (1866), Musée d'Orsay, Paris, France

6

Women in the Garden (1866), Musée d'Orsay, Paris, France

That's why Monet often
painted on a very large canvas.
This one is so big that
it is almost life-size.

Sometimes, Monet drew and painted
at even larger than life-size.
Like this.

The Woman in a Green Dress (1866),
Kunsthalle Bremen, Germany

11

Can you work out what Monet was
painting by looking at these details
from his pictures?

*"I think this is a white cloud
floating in a blue sky."*

"And I think I know this one.

It's dark clouds just before

it starts pouring with rain."

13

You are both wrong!
The first detail is white cloud
reflected in a clear pond.
When the water ripples, the clouds ripple too.

Water Lilies (1915), Musée Marmottan Monet, Paris, France

And this is not dark clouds.
It's gray smoke from a steam train.

Okay, let's try again.

"I can tell what this is straightaway.
It's a cloud turning red as the sun sets.
And the cloud is being reflected by water."

"And this looks like thin, wispy cloud
being blown along by a strong wind."

Water Lilies (1907),
private collection

Hooray!
You got this
one right.

But this is
not cloud.
It's a lady's dress
rippling in
the wind.

Do you see how
hard it is to
identify Monet's
subjects from
small details?

Woman with a Parasol (1875),
National Gallery of Art,
Washington, USA

19

Let's take a look at another
of Monet's paintings.

"Hmm. What could this be?"

"I don't have a clue!"

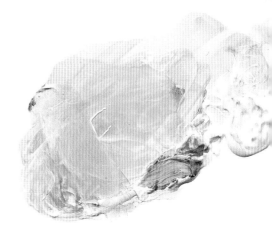

"Let's look at it all."

"Gee, it's very long!"

23

Now step back and look at the painting from a distance.

What can you see?

Water Lilies – The Clouds (1920–26), Musée de l'Orangerie, Paris, France

"Ah, I see what it is!"

"Yes, it's the sky reflected in a pond where water lilies are floating on the surface."

That's right!

So why did Monet paint pictures this way?

Haystack at Sunset, Frosty Weather (1891), private collection

Monet wanted to paint colors in nature
at different moments in time.
The light changed quickly, so he had to work fast.

He painted shapes directly onto the canvas,
covering it with many quick, overlapping strokes.

Haystacks, End of Summer (1891), Musée d'Orsay, Paris, France

Close up, you see only the brushstrokes.
But step back and view the painting from a distance,
and you will see exactly what Monet was looking at!

In Monet's paintings, sunlight pours in,
and dark shadows on water sway.

Monet's friends used to say to him,
"What an amazing eye you have
for the effects of the light."

Portrait of Claude Monet (1875)
by Pierre-Auguste Renoir,
Musée d'Orsay, Paris, France

Bathers at La Grenouillère (1869),
Metropolitan Museum of Art,
New York, USA

29

The ever-changing colors of nature

Monet was born in Paris in 1840. When he was five, his family moved to the town of Le Havre on the north coast of France. His parents ran a store there and were always busy. So Monet passed a lot of time alone and had to amuse himself. He spent many days just looking at the sea, which helped him develop an appreciation of the changing colors and patterns of nature.

The Impressionists

Monet took drawing lessons when he was at high school and studied under the painter Eugène Boudin. After his mother died in 1857, he moved to Paris. Then in 1861 he decided to join the army. He spent two years in Algeria in Africa, where he was amazed by the bright sunlight and the richness of the colors in nature. When he returned to Paris two years later, he met and began working with a group of painters including Pierre-Auguste Renoir and Camille Pissarro. These painters liked to work outdoors and tried to paint the changing effects of light on nature. Soon they became known as the Impressionists, a name that came from one of Monet's paintings, *Impression: Sunrise.*

Different shades

Early on in his life, Monet had noticed how the color of the ocean changes according to the position of the sun and the amount of cloud in the sky.

Impression: Sunrise (1873), Museé Marmottan Monet, Paris, France

1840
Monet is born in Paris, France

1845
His family moves to Le Havre on France's north coast

1859
While studying at art school in Paris, he meets painters Camille Pissarro and Gustave Courbet

1861
Joins the army and leaves for Algeria, Africa

Bathers at La Grenouillère (1869), Metropolitan Museum of Art, New York, USA

We tend to think of the ocean as always being blue, but during sunrise it may take on a red shade and when it's a cloudy day it may become a dark blue-gray.

Monet's attempts to capture the changing colors of nature resulted in paintings that looked sketchy or unfinished. Some people found this strange and criticized his work. Monet ignored their complaints and carried on working in the same way. Gradually, many painters realized how clever Monet's art was and they started using similar methods.

Monet kept painting until he died. He received little recognition for his achievements during his lifetime. But today he is one of the most famous and popular painters of all time.

Same place, another time

Although the two paintings below are of much the same subject, they are not alike. That's because the season and time of day were not the same. So the light, shade, and colors, and the overall impression the artist recorded on each occasion, are different.

Haystacks, End of Summer (1891), Musée d'Orsay, Paris, France

Haystack at Sunset, Frosty Weather (1891), private collection

1870
Marries Camille Doncieux

1879
Death of Camille

1883
Moves to the small town of Giverny, west of Paris

1926
Dies at the age of 86

Moments in time

Water Lilies (1915), Musée Marmottan Monet, Paris, France

The two paintings on this page are both by Monet and both show a pond covered with water lilies. But can you see how different they are? One was painted in the middle of the day when the sun was high in the sky. The other shows the surface of the water glowing red as the sun set. It's the colors of the clouds that indicate the time of day. The daytime clouds are white and fluffy, while the sunset clouds are yellow, orange, and red.

Monet loved to study the colors of nature. In 1883 he moved to a house with a large garden at Giverny, outside Paris. In the 1890s he bought more land and expanded the garden to include several ponds covered with water lilies. Monet spent the rest of his life observing

Water Lilies (1907), Private Collection

the effects of the sunlight on his garden and painting enormous pictures of the lily ponds. Even though he painted the same subject over and over, no two of his paintings are the same, and all are beautiful. Isn't that amazing?

The Gare Saint-Lazare: Arrival of a Train (1877), Fogg Museum, Cambridge, Massachusetts, USA

Catching the trains

For a time in the 1870s, Monet lived in an apartment next to one of Paris's largest stations, the Gare Saint-Lazare. From his window, he watched the trains come and go and became fascinated by the combined effects of the sunlight and the steam and smoke from the trains. Eventually he made a series of 12 paintings of the station. He had to work fast to paint the trains before they moved off. He would even beg the stationmaster to delay a train's departure so that he could finish a painting!

His favorite model

Monet regularly drew and painted his wife, Camille, partly because he couldn't afford to pay other models to sit for him but also because he loved to look at her. Sadly, Camille did not live long enough to see Monet become a famous artist. She passed away in 1879, at the young age of 32. Heartbroken, Monet made a final painting of Camille as she lay on her deathbed.

Woman with a Parasol (1875), National Gallery of Art, Washington, USA

"Monet's sharp eyes observed

every tiny change in the light."